SEO BASICS HANDS-ON THEORY AND PRACTICE

Theoretical and Practical Aspects of SEO

Ali Muattar

ANish Publications

Copyright © 2019 ANish Publications

All rights reserved

The characters and events portrayed in this book are fictitious. Any similarity to real persons, living or dead, is coincidental and not intended by the author.

No part of this book may be reproduced, or stored in a retrieval system, or transmitted in any form or by any means, electronic, mechanical, photocopying, recording, or otherwise, without express written permission of the publisher.

Cover design by: ANish Designs
Printed in the Islamic Republic of Pakistan

I dedicate this book to my father, my only friend who doesn't want me to give up on anything I put my mind to achieving. He is my hero and will be there for me if I need guidance. I have always relied on his advice, and he is the only one patiently waiting for my book's second edition on Amazon.

CONTENTS

Title Page
Copyright
Dedication
Chapter 1: Introduction to SEO ... 1
Chapter 2: What is SEO? ... 4
Chapter 3: Why SEO ... 6
Chapter 4: When to use SEO ... 37
Chapter 5: SEO Basics: Where to Use SEO ... 45
Chapter 6: SEO Basics: Which Type of SEO ... 48
Chapter 7: SEO Basics: How to do SEO ... 51
Chapter 8: SEO Basics: Who should do SEO? ... 54
SEO Basics Guidelines ... 55
SEO Basics Checklist ... 56
Chapter 9: Suggestions and Recommendations ... 57
Up to you, Dear Reader! ... 59
Acknowledgement ... 61
About The Author ... 63
ANish Publications' SEO series ... 65
THE END ... 67

CHAPTER 1: INTRODUCTION TO SEO

In the name of Allah, the most gracious and merciful, I started this book in January, and I wanted to give my readers the basic concepts of SEO so they can use them in their practice. Most of the advice you may be inclined to be from companies with tools for efforts to steal other people's traffic.

I have no intention of doing so. However, I am working with my technical team to build our search engine that will index content due to its context in the formulation. But that dream is yet to come; this is a long shot among 200 search engines, as per my knowledge.

I started writing this book in 2018 after spending precious years in the field juggling with SEO to leverage my share of the market. I have acquired whatever I have gained in these years. I am happily transferring to you so you can have the efficiency of your efforts with the genuine advice you need from the person worthy of your attention.

I never call myself the expert; this is what people call me, but my claim is valid only because I say I am the wager student of life that never gets tired of teaching me. I always enjoy listening to and learning it.

These are my ground realities, so before you get to the next chapter, I want to be honest with you professionally. If you are ok with it, you may proceed; otherwise, you have a lot of self-proclaimed SEO experts who are there for all their products, tools, and services. I am someone other than them.

I have learned everything from trial and error, so it is better to live with mistakes than to die with the perfection of ignorance. Hands-on theory and practice are all about the Theoretical and Practical Aspects of SEO that give you a new confidence to leverage your traffic for your benefit.

SEO Basics Hands-on Theory and Practice are worth having as a guide to boost online traffic with easy-to-use techniques. I love basics because they give you the stepping stone to lay your foundation on solid rock so nothing can shake your foundations. Changes in time and strategies will not affect you as much as others may be affected. So, here is everything I have to say to you.

Basics are those units of structure and functions of anything; nothing can remain with accuracy and effectiveness without them. Although the field is expanding, SEO is not an exception, and hundreds of more indicators are added and removed from search engines. However, there are still those basics that remain basic no matter how the area changes.

Basics start with opened ended questions; the name indicates once you start, it will tell you everything you need to know about the topic you are solving with these questions. Fortunately, we have two questions in English: open-ended and closed-ended.

The open-ended questions are also called Wh- questions. These questions explain everything to a person about a topic. The closed-ended questions are Yes and No questions. They are not intended to answer or explain the subject entirely but to confirm the facts and figures.

In most cases, they only need one word to answer; sometimes, a nod or a gesture can replace these words if you see the person you want to ask your closed-ended questions. You can add details to these yes and no questions.

Generally, open-ended questions start with "Wh" except for how; these are what, why, when, where, which, how, and who.

In the following chapters, we will discuss each SEO topic with these fundamental questions and answer them with theory and practical aspects of the past, current knowledge, and future insights.

But before that, I will try to discuss this SEO with you, so the following topics are not confusing, and I will try my best not to bore you with the technicality of this topic as you have seen self-proclaimed gurus saying anything about this topic without confronting the fundamental questions that any intelligent student ask about the SEO.

CHAPTER 2: WHAT IS SEO?

When I ask this question during interviews, classes, seminars, workshops, and WP Boot camps from beginners, intermediate, and advanced level SEO professionals, most keep quiet, and few say something. Still, these are not the answers to my questions. These are the answers of self-proclaimed SEO experts who manipulated SEO and increased their visibility on the World Wide Web.

But I am sorry to say they have one agenda to grow their business, sell their software, online programs, classes, seminars, and subscription-based platforms. If you expect genuine advice from these experts, you must check your mental status, my friend. I don't like sleazy salespeople; they want to sell me things I don't need or want. If I need anything, I will buy it; I don't need a salesperson to tell me what to buy.

When you want to learn something, you must ask these questions, which are not selling these things, but they are doing it. I will not ask about SEO from those selling products and related services. I will ask those who are doing SEO and are not selling it but doing it to help people search for their information most accessible, **accessible**, and convenient.

The public is not interested in buying SEO; they are interested in the information. The best, most reliable, and valid information is needed for user satisfaction. Fancy tactics, SEO manipulation, and checking mindsets threaten Search Engines and SEO, and finally, the public, in this case, the user.

Keeping this in mind, now let's talk about SEO. The name SEO is the abbreviation of three words Search Engine Optimization.

Search is derived from the Latin verb **circare**, meaning "to go around." The engine is from the Latin word **Ingenium**, meaning creation, begetting the ability of a person, place, or thing that can create something or do something new; genetics is also one of variation that is the source of all biological creations. Finally, optimization is also derived from the Latin word **Optimus**, translating as "the best," meaning that searching for engine optimization is the best way to create something for going around something.

I explained earlier that search engine optimization, or simply SEO is all about doing your best to provide the information they need for the queries they type in search engines.

What is a search engine?

The search engine is the middleware available to the public to search for their information; in other words, it is the database made with care and is for public use to explore their information and do whatever they want to do with it.

The search engine companies register under the informational technology categories in their respective legal localities because they are IT companies, and they store, retrieve, and propagate information to users and from your users to their interested parties, including governments, INGOs, NGOs, international and national agencies, advertisers, corporations, MNCs, and interest groups.

Here I want your attention to another essential aspect we will deal with in this book: the difference between data and information. Data is raw information that can be used or discarded, while information can be discarded. Valid and reliable data changes into information, which is the power in the personal, professional, and business world.

Applied knowledge is the collection of all applicable information. Research is the process of collecting data and converting it into information. The information is here to rule since the birth of human beings and will govern the existence of the human species. Only information led from the prehistoric to the current informational age; all other data forms have died in history and its arena.

So, SEO is the use of accurate data and changing it to information consumed by the user, and the user will act upon this information to solve real-world problems. Now it is apparent what SEO is, it is time to move to our next question in the following chapter: Why SEO?

CHAPTER 3: WHY SEO

This question is all about its importance;

Why Seo?

To give your user the best experience they expect from your knowledge and expertise.

They need information; you give them the best possible ways to have that information, and that is it. The SEO part is now finished, and all other things come in the form after this. Now you can educate and entertain your users after giving them information. You need relevant information to do the two.

For Analytics

SEO is your number one tool to measure your effectiveness online.

It is your measurable asset where you can do many things to ensure what works for you and what doesn't. But excluding your SEO can lead you to lose powerful tools to get into your analytics. Almost all aspects of SEO can be measured, reported, and monitored, but most of the things in web development, designing, writing, marketing, branding, etc.

It can't be measured accurately. We also depend on SEO metrics to know whether our processes work. So, SEO is the core fundamental for online and offline success and failure, and that's why we need it to do it efficiently.

Suggestions To Do Better In Your Seo Strategy Analytics:

Do It;

Where to use SEO?

This question is one of the basics that beginners, intermediate, and advanced-level SEOs ask me whenever I come in contact with them. And my answer always includes one of the following aspects of SEO strategy:

- Set one particular time or day in the week to work on your analytics
- Choose the best platform to deliver everything you want to see in your analytics
- Get the experts' advice on your specific goals and visions
- Ask help from your fellow SEOs to teach or train you for a better understanding of your analytics.
- Show your team and everyone contributing to your SEO the results of their hard work and dedication.
- Reward the small victories of your team by achieving a specific target
- Never stop the flow of communication among your team members
- Restrict unwanted access of team members not contributing to your SEO strategy
- Report clearly and save it for future use

Don't Do It:

- Checking analytics each time you are free
- Choosing every platform that you can lay your hands on without relying on one best platform
- Doing everything by yourself without consulting other experts in the field
- Never asking for help and turning a cold ear to the help others give you directly or

indirectly
- Never sharing your results with your team responsible for SEO success and failure
- Not rewarding those who have out-performed in your SEO success story
- Concealing communication and breaking its flow either from upside down or downside upwards.
- Allowing everyone to access your analytics
- Neither reporting nor having any backups of your success or failure SEO strategy analytics.

For Authority

SEO show authority; it doesn't matter whether you are a beginner or seasoned SEO professional if you are doing great work by contributing to your specific field. SEO makes you a thought leader because the public follows those who contribute something back to the community.

I am a psychology student having an Entrepreneurial journey, but if you search my name in any search engine you have installed on your operating system.

Your search will tell you a lot about me and indicate me as a thought leader in psychology, writing, and entrepreneurship; why? Because of this SEO, I am regarded as an authority on psychology, writing, marketing, business, mental health, and expert authorship worldwide through online publications like Amazon and ANish Publications.

The more you give back to the community, the more you are regarded as an authority in the field. My focus has been on cyber security, SEO, and IT for more than 14+ years of trial and error and stumbling. So, Why SEO; because it boosts your authority worldwide and in your social circles.

Suggestions To Do Better In Your Seo Strategy For Authority:

Do It;

- Research your topic well and do your best to provide excellent content to your users
- Write when you think you can do it better
- Edit your content before it is published
- Format for any errors, typos, and mistakes that can be made before publishing to the world
- Grammar checks your content before publication. Authority comes with fewer mistakes and errors only known to the experts; general users don't find it even if they read your content for the hundredth time.
- Proofread before publishing your piece of content because once it is published, it is gone
- Never miss the opportunity to learn and relearn from other authority figures in your field of interest.

Don't Do It:

- Passing comments neither researched nor accepted in your field
- Writing whatever comes into your mind to tell search engines that you are creating something daily
- Editing only when it is already published and messing with the format and overall structure and design of your content
- Formatting when users tell you about them
- Never bother grammar because you think your user's average reading capacity is 8th grade, and they don't care about grammar.
- Proofreading looks childish to you because this is not print media where one typing mistake can make you guilty of being the victim and vice versa
- Learning is not for you because you are an expert, and experts must teach only

For Availability

SEO is a process of hard work and dedication to your craft, so it is available to each person and individual; that is why people invest in SEO. Whether a teenage sophomore, undergraduate, graduate, or postgraduate, you have the equal opportunity to get the best result from your SEO efforts.

Availability is the global currency that is making this field open to industry-specific niche beginners and advanced-level professionals to have the best possible outcomes you seek from your skillset and mindset to set for your success in the online world.

Whether I am talking to school-age students, my message is the same: the world has plenty of resources, and we all have to choose the ones we like. The availability of SEO gives a chance for doing it at the first chance to make an impact instantly.

Suggestions To Do Better In Your Seo Strategy For Availability:

Do It;

- Use this availability wisely because it is not available to you but to all those website owners who want to use it
- Availability doesn't mean that you are allowed to do whatever you want to do in your SEO strategy; you are bound to learn the basics and abide by it
- Misuse of it can backfire

- Time and space matter in this area too
- Finding the best tools to help you work on your SEO strategy to make a mark on your online presence and branding processes.

Don't Do It:

- Thinking that SEO is only available to you and no one else will use its power to surpass you in everything you offer to your users and clients worldwide and locally.
- Believing that you can do whatever you want with your SEO strategy to fool your users and search engines.
- There are no consequences for playing the devil and expecting angelic results from search engines and your users
- You have freedom of space and time online
- No tools can help you to enhance the SEO strategy; you have to find a one-person army for your brand and the online survival

For Branding

Branding is a marketing method that uses psychological ways to give your users everything they need to know about you, your business, your goals, dreams, and ambitions. You can't make adjustments once your branding has been done successfully.

Although rebranding is common practice, unicorn companies never choose this risky path because if it goes wrong, everything is lost in minutes. SEO is the best tool for branding locally and worldwide, and you can tell your users what your vision is and how you are doing your best to achieve your goals and realize your dreams.

Branding without SEO is a fancy desire, and the time had gone when people did it without the internet. Still, at the end of the 20th century and the beginning of the 21st century, you can't even imagine you can get what you want in branding without turning your gears on SEO.

Why not use SEO to improve your branding strategies to reach more people searching for you and your products and services? This usability makes a case for a successful SEO strategy to execute and promote your branding.

Suggestions To Do Better In Your Seo Strategy For Branding:

Do It;

- Stay consistent with your message and its delivery
- Get the best insights from experts in the field to make your brand stand out from the crowd
- Make your voice and avoid copy-paste culture
- Make close attention to your branding strategy, especially your branding physical appearance, color psychology, typography, and graphic design
- Show them, don't tell

Don't Do It:

- Be like a flying bee and create your message as you go; change it whenever you want to and deliver your message to all those not interested in you or your brand
- No need to get expert insights, but do what you like to do to copy the same strategy other brands in your niche used to succeed
- Specific voice is a waste of time and energy; steal others' tags and titles and create your universe around them
- Work on your SEO strategy no need to worry about your physical branding appearance online because SEO alone can get you your desired results
- Nothing to show; tell and expect the best results without working for them in any aspect

For Clickability

Everything that clicks the mind and hearts of users will live long; connecting is the currency of online business these days. Even people have services for business owners and website owners to give them a certain number of clicks, and they will charge for it instantly.

Clickability is the valuable asset a website has in each search engine. The more clicks you receive, the more chance you get to reach people's hearts and minds. Remember that you receive clicks only when you have all the best SEO practices on your site to amaze your user.

This point is vague without the best practices ensured on your websites. It would help if you worked on your SEO to improve your clickability; doing it right makes you near your business and professional goals.

Here is the best case for SEO in your hand; again, you will reach your optimum heights from search engine searching queries only when you implement everything you know about SEO and are open to doing the right thing at the right time.

Suggestions To Do Better In Your Seo Strategy For Clickability:

Do It;

- Write psychological headlines and entice the emotional minds of your users but never lose contact with the logical mind
- Clickbait will work best for a short time, but in the long run, it will harm your online reputation
- Fooling search engines will cost you too much to bear along with your ranking, users, and indexing
- Be genuine and say what you know and do what you say; never contradict your saying and doing online
- Misuse of users' psychology can hurt your efforts more than enhancing your clickability rates
- Clickability is not the only success key to your success; your bounce rate, engagement, shares, comments, and other social proofs have a lot to do with it.
- Double-check your clickability. Is it genuine, or is it accidental?
- Play at the safer side of the SEO game plan; avoid clickability scams and schemes
- Be ethical in your clickability rates and responses to them.

Don't Do It:

- Never let your users' psychology tract them to your content
- Investing in clickbait to increase your click-through rates and regarding your self the king of the online world
- Fooling search engines with the keywords, phrases, and titles of other languages to draw traffic in and make an impression to earn a better place in ranking and indexing
- Fake it until you make it mean that you do your best to lie to your users about a subject matter and expect genuine traffic.
- Play with the minds of your users who think that you are giving them accurate information and playing with their health, wealth, and especially mental health
- Promoting your products and services with hidden charges and terms and conditions to rob them of their money and eventually being sued by them in the legal systems.

- Taking your clickability rates as your only goal for success in your SEO strategy, all other things like bounce rate, engagement, and user upvotes have no value in your eyes.
- Participating in clickbait schemes and paying for shady practices in SEO to achieve your goal of visitors and users without working on your content to produce better quality and high value for the users by visiting your site.

For Competition

Although I don't believe in competition, this western concept of competition exists in local and international markets whether you believe it or not. Online Sharks are there to steal or copy your strategy no matter what you do to protect your business secrets from your competition.

Your title tags, keywords, and overall SEO strategies can be hacked through much online proprietary software, and your competitors can use it on their websites too.

Although it is not ethical, pragmatic philosophies of the West and Machiavellian politics of the West and the East can make it moral as long the ends satisfy the means. Competition exists in local and international markets, and its denial is only preferable for some, including me.

So, I assume you believe it, or if you do not think it, you must keep in mind that the internet is full of hackers stealing people's strategies to enhance their ideas, products, and services; it is a common practice no matter what you do to counter it.

All legal procedures have failed. Examples include but are not limited to copyright acts, patent rights, trademarks, governmental registrations, DMCA, EU's GDPR, US's COPA, and watermarks, to name a few. Still, your competition does it without considering the consequences of breaching the ethical consideration of national and international laws and regulations.

The only refuge you have to counter this unethical competition is using the best practices and general guidelines search engines and organizations put forward to help you do the right thing in SEO.

Once you understand that your game at SEO is the game changer, you will always be different. Get back and improve your strategy and do it again and never stop because once you stop your SEO journey, you are prey to your competition, and they will hunt you down, tired and feared.

Suggestions to do better in your Competitive SEO Strategy:

Do It;

- Research your competition as much as possible; I have gone through this today. Once I discovered my competition, I had to x-ray my competitors' online and offline resources, including their blogs and websites. I have their data from 2005 to date. However, I don't suggest you do that because I have found through my experience that it doesn't work that much, but at that time, it looked important, so I did it. I had everything about them, yet they haven't done that for me. If we were in the same ring to fight for our success in the internet arena, I would beat them in two blows because I know everything about them; but they don't have anything about me or my business. This research is an edge, and it's also an advantage.
- Understand their motivations and inspirations.
- Understand their processes, meaning what they are doing and how they are doing that very thing.
- Know about your blind spots: Identify your strengths as well as your weaknesses
- Create content that attracts your users to you
- Leverage the power of social media for your content promotion
- Get your links from high-authority websites
- Always check your progress via analytics tools you have decided for your platform, and never postpone it; the day you forget to do it, you are sidetracked
- Optimization of your website is a must; you must keep an eye out for better results and rankings
- Update your content regularly. I update my blogs from 2003 till this date because I love them so do my readers. Once you stop updating, your game is over; keep this in mind.
- Trial and error are the rules of the SEO world; experiment with your SEO strategy but never go too far and come back to each SEO's success formula, which shows results to them whenever they apply it. See for yourself what works for you and what doesn't.

Don't Do It:

- Black hat SEO is not for success; it is a quick fix, and you will be punished even if you stop doing it. See it as karma; you do well, receive well, and receive bad if you do wrong. I haven't seen one SEO who succeeded in fooling search engines in forever. If you have met one or you are the one, I would love to hear from you. So, do it ever even if you see no progress in your organic traffic or months or years
- Spam is for spammers, and they don't get far in this business. Link building is a

failed strategy; you will get it sooner or later.
- Keyword stuffing is your worst enemy neither your users nor your search engine bots like and admires it. So please don't do it ever.
- Cloaking is your worst enemy; get back from doing it
- Hidden texts are a terrible practice; refrain from their use
- Doorway pages are for the immature get-up and be mature to get the best deal for your SEO strategy
- Never engage in link buying and selling schemes, including automated link building and artificial link juice schemes; they will get you busted in no time
- Ethics are the core fundamentals; never back down from your ethical SEO strategy. Being honest is the only strategy I know to help you get results.

For Connectivity

SEO connects you with your users, which is the best thing to happen to you. Connection is the first step to everything; if your users are not connected to you, no matter what you do, you can't achieve what you deserve with your SEO. The efforts you make to make your mark on the hearts and minds of your user is the valuable asset an individual or group have at their box to go high in the search engine and the users' visibility.

I am a vocal advocate of connectivity worldwide; until and unless you are connected to your user, you can't do anything. Your user can only find you once and if you leverage the help of applicable SEO. So, part of the equation is to do the best online, you must work on connectivity to your users, and your users can only find you if you are connecting them with your brand through SEO best practices.

You will lead your company by example if you stick to the best efforts of SEO to help you get connections with your users, and those users connect you to more users; these chain reactions create miracles in the online businesses and lives of successful brands worldwide. So another way is connectivity, which is how you use SEO for better connections with your users.

Suggestions to do better in your Connectivity SEO Strategy:

Do It;

- Choose relevant keywords for your topics

- Research your topics deeply
- Use your keywords in your titles, body contents, and a section dedicated to your tags
- Social media is your first choice for users' connectivity; use it wisely
- Create blogs and articles around your tags, not tags around your blogs; stuffing is a terrible practice in the online SEO community
- Backlink with those who link you too; otherwise, it is a waste of time
- Analytics is your friend; get insights about your traffic here
- SEO tools are your helping hands; get plenty of help from them in your SEO strategy
- Having fresh content in at least one blog per week is good practice; don't get too lazy to write one blog per week. Search engines and users love fresh content, so continuously create it for your connectivity with your users.

Don't Do It:

- Don't ignore your website design: Your website's overall design is your users' first connection with you. Humans are a visually dominant species, so design your website on your first chance. Poor design scares your users, and they will fly away from it.
- Don't rely on desktops; mobile is winning the battle now: Optimize your website for mobile devices because the dominant user base is browsing the internet over the mobile phone; you will be disappointed if your website is not optimized for mobile responsiveness.
- Don't dwell over your website speed: slow websites have a greater rate of bounce back of users
- Not claiming your listings on local directories and review sites the best tenant of local SEO
- Don't invest time writing attractive meta descriptions to attract users from SERPs.
- Not adding alt text to your images to have better results in image search directories and search engines
- Not creating fresh and unique content for users and search engines
- Not using social media: I did not use social media for content promotion; I made this mistake, but once I got it, I never looked back again.
- Not analyzing your efforts and progress regularly.

For Cooperation

Cooperation is the mutual respectful way of connection that I love and believe in business and life. Instead of competition, cooperation can do well for both parties. SEO is all about cooperation; a genuine helping hand to support each other in delivering the best possible information to the users and then passing them to your cooperation to see more valuable information on another website or resource center of another company or organization. That is when your backlinking helps do the best for your user, your cooperation, and yourself.

SEO helps you pave the foundations of cooperation between you and other individuals and groups to serve your user the best experience they deserve and desire. Once you get into collaboration, you will leverage excellent opportunities for yourself and others through guiding principles of SEO and practical usage of it. Good luck with this aspect of why SEO.

Suggestions to do better in your Cooperation SEO Strategy:

Do It;

- Spot your key players in your field and industry (excluding me and other authors' authority in your area!) and cooperate with them to do better; they will do the same. Cooperation can be achieved through guest blogging, interviewing, and sharing their content on your platforms and social media. Remember one psychological fact: serious attention and sincere admiration are never wasted; you can read the history and find the genuine side of this claim I made.
- Improve the quality of your content people like us will cooperate more and fast than you think
- Instead of competition, promote a cooperation culture in the online world; believe me, you will learn something new and fulfilling that can't be learned through competition
- Be friendly with your fellow SEOs and your users; no one like the lectures of a professor all day long. Entice humor in your content now and then to break the ice of rapport and connection, which are the first steps of cooperation among human beings.
- Engage in the local gathering of SEOs to cooperate with other professionals in your local community and forums online for your SEO strategy.

Don't Do It:

- Shying away from linking out other websites and blogs
- Not using social media to use it for your SEO; most of the traffic I receive on my website is through my social media platform profile clicks. You can do it too for your success.
- Neglecting critical influencers in your niche; be cautious, though don't engage in

paid cooperation; they will not get you anywhere. I didn't do it, so I can't suggest it to you.
- Creating everything for dominant search engines, I know more than 200, including our project. So if you are focusing on one or two search engines, you are ignoring other search engines that may be a hub for your target users and influencers.

For Cost Ability

Whether self-finance or business finance at a larger scale, you must check your costs and income to decide whether you are doing your best to grow your brand and website through SEO. If you do it right and cost-effectively, you can invest your money in something else to grow and scale your business.

Cost ability is one of your limitations; if you have little money, you can still choose to invest it wisely. SEO helps you lower the cost of costly advertising and marketing on print and electronic media, either paid or on your own.

The more you control your cost ability, the more you are successful in making profits. You need users to come to your website so you can lead them everywhere you want to show. You can guide them to download your free giveaway, sign up for your newsletter, get membership, or participate in your survey to help you serve them better with better products and services.

You can navigate them to your sales funnel; you can give them the option to be an insider of your robust forum and community of their interest. This and much more can be possible if you use the best SEO methods to achieve your desired outcomes. Giving you a chance to get the best feature of SEO for your why SEO question.

Suggestions to do better in your Cost ability SEO Strategy:

Do It;

- Keep your costs in check
- Invest in your cost-effective keywords and strategies
- Invest in your research tools for SEO
- Involve and engage in social media that is a relatively cost-able platform for your SEO

- Follow search engines' best practices and submit your website to web directories
- Earn quality links and monitor their progress

Don't do it:

- Don't ignore your costability
- Don't fool yourself over backlinks worth to your SEO strategy
- Don't rely on one search engine to optimize your website for different search engines, platforms, and screen sizes.
- Don't undermine optimizing your website for mobile

For Credibility

Credibility is developed through hard work, dedication, and stumbling. But you build credibility if you are persistent enough to deliver the best results despite what others say about you and your brand or website. Credibility is a long journey, and you must devise a plan to give your users credible information, so they start believing your credibility.

This journey must be a source of your motivation to be a credible source of information for your users. Now hundreds of search engines prefer to rank those sources higher in their indexing and search results which people trust, and their credibility is higher compared to other sources. SEO makes this journey exciting yet challenging because once you are after credibility, you cannot fool users with thin content, trendy topics, click baits, or something like that.

You will research deeply to produce an epic piece of content that can make your credibility more prominent to your users and search engines. You can't follow or copy-paste others' ideas if you want to be a credible source of information for both search engines and your users. This aspect of SEO is worth mentioning: you must use SEO to build credibility among the online community interested in your interest.

Suggestions to do better in your Credibility SEO Strategy:

Do It;

- Well, research your topic before publications
- Produce quality content; update and optimize regularly

- Promote via social media and other media platforms
- Stay connected to your field's current research and discoveries

Don't Do It:

- Don't rely on one source for your research and topic selection
- Don't put all your content in one category
- Don't rely on one search engine for your traffic; diversify your horizon of optimization
- Don't forget your user experience and engagement with your content and overall website design and aesthetics
- Don't ignore the speed of your website and blogs.

For Effectivity

SEO is the most exciting part of search engines that affects both engines and users. The effectiveness is measured through users' stay on the web page or bounce backs. The more your users stay on your website, the more you are using the effective ways and best practices of SEO.

Effectiveness comes from honesty, genuine content, and helpful information; if you are engaging in shady SEO practices that boost your search ranking but eventually you get caught in the maze of effectiveness tests each search engine implements to vet out the bad players and help those players who play with the rules and provide everything to their users.

Effectiveness is one of the essential aspects of SEO; you work for the search engine feeding it everything it needs to categorize your content for users and users to get the best of their online experience. I am a fan of SEO effectiveness because it doesn't matter how hard you work to write your fantastic blog for your users, who will love reading it and implementing it in their personal and professional lives.

You have to optimize it for a search engine to know your intent and users' intent to match their searches. When both objectives meet, this is your golden chance to reach your target audience. The following way for your SEO is effectiveness and then efficiency.

Suggestions to do better in your Effectivity SEO Strategy:

Do It;

- Select your target users and keywords that they are looking and searching for to have a fantastic experience online
- Research your competitions/cooperation (depends on your mindset and which one resonates with your mind and current realities)
- Define your quality standards and never bypass them in any regard
- Adjust your SEO strategy regularly to meet the needs of your growth curve
- Open your mind and eyes to the latest SEO trends

Don't Do It:

- Don't overuse your keywords in your website content
- Don't stuff keywords; never repeat and replicate your keywords
- Don't use too general and specific keywords
- Don't use a long-tailed keyword if not necessary
- Don't use keywords if there are spelling or grammatical mistakes in them

For Efficiency

SEO boosts your efficiency when you start implementing it and see instant results after a few days and months. The mathematical nature of SEO gives it the power of efficiency to get the best results you want from your strategy.

This efficiency will be further discussed when discussing the how part of SEO. But here, my core point is that one of the most vital aspects of the usage of SEO is its efficiency, and if you want efficient results, you must work on your SEO first; all other things come after it.

Suggestions to do better in your Efficiency SEO Strategy:

Do It;

- Pay close attention to your website loading speed; even the milliseconds count in an online world
- Invest your efforts in optimizing title tags and meta descriptions; they will help you in the long run
- Use keywords wisely in your content, if possible in your images too
- Schema markup will do the best for your SEO strategy, so implement it as soon as possible.
- Promote your content on multiple platforms, including social media and niche-specific groups and communities
- Start focusing on quality link-building strategies
- Research, monitor, and adjust your keyword research

Don't Do It:

- Don't use automated bots to help you in your SEO strategy
- Don't deceive your users with the information, education, and entertainment
- Don't compromise on the quality of your content
- Don't get discouraged if you don't see the results you want to see instantly

For Feasibility

SEO is feasible because you don't need a team of professionals to do it for you. It would be best to do it without wasting a penny on infrastructure to leverage results. This concept means you can do it with whatever you have instead of waiting for investors to invest in your projects.

Your website or forum, store, page, and products and services can grow with your efforts to improve and enhance your SEO strategy. Feasibility is another factor in making an SEO case.

Suggestions to do better in your Feasibility SEO Strategy:

Do It;

- Identify your target user and topic of expertise
- Stay updated on your industry's best practices and research
- Repeat your process of success regularly to move forward

Don't Do It:

- Avoid difficult keywords: Choose keywords according to your expertise and the reading capabilities of your ideal average user
- Avoid challenging, competitive, and irrelevant keywords to rank for in search engines
- Don't use emotionally charged and stop words in your keywords, title tags, and meta descriptions

For Indexing

Crawling is the mechanical part of search engine bots that work endlessly to deliver your content to your users instantly. Still, indexing is the visible part of this effort search engine bots have done patiently. SEO helps you and bots index your webpage to your user waiting for your content because they are searing for the same content you provide.

If you don't implement the best SEO practices, you will never get the results you need to index your webpage for your target users. So, part of the equation here is that you must use the power of SEO to index your page to see the results you want to watch through your efforts to help search engine bots rank your page as soon as possible.

Suggestions to do better in your Indexing SEO Strategy:

Do It;

- Create fresh content and submit your URLs to the search engines you receive traffic
- The quality link internally and externally helps you in your indexing
- Always follow the best practices for indexing your content in any search engine you wish to index your website in

Don't Do It:

- Don't try to play with the algorithm of search engines that will get you busted in no time
- Don't get in penalization by search engines
- Don't ignore title tags, quality of content, and backlink profile
- Don't ignore internal and external link opportunities
- Avoid content and link duplication
- Don't let your content lay there untouched, update or delete old content if it makes sense

For Lead Generation

Lead generation is a powerful tool that keeps your website and business alive online; once you get into the game of generating leads, you can only expect to do it with the help of SEO. Lead generation is not a joke; you will make a living with it; apart from advertising and marketing, your SEO will help you in many aspects that will make you glad.

Although it is not theoretical and reasonable, only practice can show my claims' validity. Otherwise, you can prove me wrong or right if I say that I must have Profs in front of me, so I suggest you practice it and see your results with your SEO efforts and strategies.

Suggestions to do better in your Lead Generation SEO Strategy:

Do It;

- Write titles and meta descriptions with your keywords
- Work on your headings and subheadings to be consistent with your keywords
- Optimize for Search Engine rich snippets; that way, you can generate leads fast
- Anchor texts must be the keywords that you have selected for your strategy

Don't Do It:

- Deceiving your users and potential customers
- Don't use hats altogether; they will lead you nowhere in the long run
- Don't create doorway pages, and never do cloaking, unintentional redirects
- Don't do spammy guest posting, comment spams, link exchange, automated queries to search engines

For Market Research

Market research is a worthy aspect of your SEO, and it is one of the essential aspects that makes your SEO possible; SEO, in turn, makes your market research easy. Market research and SEO are directly proportional, meaning doing one will enhance the other's power, strategy, and efficiency.

Staying on top of your market is only possible by continuous research and smelling your CHEESE regularly; the concept I borrowed from the book discussed is "Who moved my cheese?" Those individuals and businesses periodically research their market and adjust their strategies to put a dent in the universe.

Suggestions to do better in your Market Research SEO Strategy:

Do It;

- Your market research analysis of the market and your skillset and mindset are the must-do actions you can't keep on hold. We did it in one of our tech startups years ago, which led us to lose our money and people's money, and we had a lot of emotional and psychological turmoil. Now I believe that without watching and researching your market, don't ever start anything online or offline.
- Identify and select your research tools and use them in your market research efficiently and effectively.
- Ask for and look for the top performers in your field and analyze their strategy and learn from them to succeed in the game you are a part of too
- Use social media for marketing your market and the people attached to it
- Monitor market research trends on relevant blogs and community forums where your ideal users go for information, education, and entertainment
- Never compromise over your quality of content; quantity can be managed with time and effort, but quality can't be addressed in the long run

- Publish on the regular time and meet the expectation of your ideal user
- Publish and engage on other relevant blogs, forums, and social media friends and followers
- Monitor and adjust your strategy on the regular basis

Don't Do It:

- Avoid relying on one source or an unauthentic source of market research
- Avoid assumptions about your markets without research. I have done this quite a lot. I have taken a hard lesson in this regard. So, never follow the crowd; excel in your research skills
- Don't ignore the secondary sources for your market research
- Don't ignore your market's requirements, consumer behavior, demographics, psychographics, geography, etc.

For Marketing

Marketing is one of the fundamental aspects and factors of SEO you need. SEO is a cost-effective, efficient, and effective marketing source for your website and online platform. It would be best if you had not the budget to champion your expertise but one sound strategy to boost your marketing to invest in other aspects like advertising and branding and leave the core marketing field to SEO via content, social, influential, inspirational, and online marketing.

You can only do marketing with taking help from your SEO. So, get it straight and invest in your SEO strategy among your teams and projects as soon as possible to reap the benefits you can from your marketing via SEO.

Suggestions to do better in your Marketing SEO Strategy:

Do It;

- Market whenever possible your products and services but within ethical grounds
- Please start with the why of your vision then everything else will take care of themselves
- Research your market before starting and doing your marketing
- Enhance your marketing capabilities by using social media groups and communi-

ties to have an impact on your field and your users
- Market with cooperation in mind competition is not for mature and grown-ups
- Market wherever you see an opportunity

Don't Do It:

- Don't overdo marketing until and unless you appear as a sleazy salesperson
- Please don't do it when the place is not appropriate
- Please don't do it when the time is not right
- Don't market when your users are not interested
- Please don't get discouraged with first No and rejections; get used to it. I have a secret disclaimer formula and No for my products and services. Before I got accepted, I had to go to 10 places and meet ten potential clients and customers. Online my threshold is tenfold. I got rejected 99 times before I was accepted in the online arena. Be a warrior and prepare yourself for plenty of No and rejections.

For Organic Traffic

The most important aspect of SEO is that it is unpaid and organic in the digital world. Search engines earn revenues from multiple streams, including but not limited to showing results for paid ads; SEO is the organic source of your users' visits to your site.

This concept is essential to note that you get your potential customers and clients for your products and services via organic traffic, and you are paying a penny to the search engines or other platforms to send traffic to your website. The critical takeaway is that to enhance your ranking and online traffic; you must implement an SEO strategy to achieve your goals.

Suggestions to do better in your Organic traffic SEO Strategy:

Do It;

- Enhance your users' positive experience and engagement in your website by creating excellent content and using relevant keywords
- Improve the quality of links and backlinks to and from authoritative websites
- Write psychological titles and user-specific descriptions
- Invest your time in better anchor texts
- Write your best metatags as if you are writing an epic blog for your upcoming

- annual event
- Get your filenames and file paths with your keywords
- Work the same way on your pages, too, as you are working on blogs and images
- Your sitemaps must have your keywords to see results in the search engines
- Robots.txt files must include keywords for traffic attraction and maintain

Don't do it:

- Don't engage in link bait
- Link farms are forbidden, and you must refrain from them altogether
- Use black hat tactics to receive traffic

For Promotion

Online promotions boost your ranking, organic visibility, traffic, and more. This promotion can only be achieved with the help of SEO. SEO is cost-effective, so you can do it with whatever you have; it doesn't need specialized knowledge or skill set. The more you do it, the more you promote your brand, website, and platform; this is another aspect of your usage of SEO.

Suggestions to do better in your Promotion SEO Strategy:

Do It;

- Optimize for the right keywords, tags, and descriptions
- Promote your content through social media
- Fix SEO issues the moment you encounter them. Don't let your users contact you to do it
- Use analytics to see your results and the progress of your promotion

Don't Do It:

- Don't promote if you haven't optimized your website for suitable keywords, tags, and descriptions
- Don't promote on social media if you can't accept negative criticism
- Don't ignore your SEO errors and resolve them if they are from your server side or your side; your themes, plugins, and forms are the reason.

- Don't be lazy to check your analytics and tools to help you identify issues on your website and report you instantly.

For Ranking

The ranking is affected by SEO, and it is one of the vital parts of SEO success and failure. Even I have seen many companies and organizations that regularly monitor the ranking of their products and services online along with their overall order of a website. My point here is that different search engines have various factors in ranking websites, so you should be disappointed by this fact.

Although ranking is necessary, it is not the overall success of your SEO strategy and game plan. My suggestion is to monitor weekly stats rather than dwelling over daily ranking up and downs and evaluate what could be done to improve your ranking and then stick to the best practice of SEO you have implemented previously to rank relatively better and be open to new learning to produce the best results you wish to see.

Suggestions to do better in your SEO Strategy:

Do It;

- Work on your website's overall design and navigation; if they are doing best, your ranking is inevitable
- Use the best practices of SEO to create an epic journey for a user to land on your website, and the time passes by, they feel that they must stay here more
- Write better content
- Optimize your images
- Try to use your pictures, not the free ones
- Select better tools to perfect your content
- Write, edit, grammar check, and then publish
- Write at least 2500 words per page or blog that will take at least 15 minutes to read
- Your minimum rate for a user to read your content should be five to 7 minutes; busy users don't have more time, but the dedicated user will spend 15 minutes on your blog and pages

Don't Do It:

- Don't ignore the power of a great design of your content, website, and images
- Don't ignore the best practices of SEO
- Don't forget to write better content weekly
- Don't overdo your design; that will backfire
- Don't misuse tools that can create buzz for you and your content
- Don't forget to set your minimum and maximum to fit your strategy
- Don't over or under-estimate your user attention span
- Don't get discouraged if you don't see instant results

For Speed In Deliverability

If you ask me what the first thing that clicks my mind to go further on any website is, I will answer speed. Speed is the deliverability of your content and, as a result, your products and services to your users. I expect your website to deliver the content of my interest when I search for it in your search bar.

The same is valid with all other users; we are in a hurry; the seconds you put us on wait, the higher chances of our bounce back. Suppose you are genuinely interested in your speed and deliverability of content. Work on the speed parameters of your website to kick-start your SEO strategy.

Suggestions to do better in your SEO Strategy:

Do It;

- Leverage the help of CDN like cloud fare etc.
- Work on your image optimization
- Work hard on your HTTP requests
- Please select the best and most lightweight caching plugin, but before doing it, ask your hosting providers whether they allow that specific plugin on their platform's domains and hosting plans.
- Invest your efforts in minifying and loading CSS and JS files
- Work on your database optimizations; this way, you can get the best results in the long run
- Change your hosting service providers, giving you a slower server to load slowly. The pro tip is to buy your hosting from local or relatively small hosting companies

because these companies strive to provide you with 99% uptime and faster-hosting servers. After all, they have fewer websites on their servers, so they ensure its proper management uptime. More prominent companies have a more extensive client base; they don't care about customer care.
- Use the power of responsive design and psychological headlines

Don't Do It:

- Please don't ignore your website speed; it will ensure a better user experience and better engagement ratio
- Monitor and analyze your website speed at different times on the regular basis

For Success In Seo

Success is a subjective experience; some objective aspects of the arena of SEO include organic traffic, increased engagement, ROI, lead generation, click-through rates, and much more that can be attributed to SEO strategy. SEO success generally means better results in your expected and achieved goals and motivations. No one parameter can be attached to SEO success, and it's subjective, so different people have different experiences and expectations regarding their success.

Suggestions to do better in your Success SEO Strategy:

Do It;

- Ensure that your content has well-researched data and relevant keywords to target your users
- Select tools and services to help you in your SEO success
- Keep updated and optimized content on your website and discard the outdated content
- Adjust, adapt, and change your strategy for better success opportunities

Don't Do It:

- Avoid affiliate links that are not serving you the best; it is handing over your customers to others
- Don't make your website the dump site of your thoughts and reasons
- Get the best content and read books to write better content for your users
- Don't use pop-ups, making it difficult for your users to focus on your content

For Genuine Traffic

SEO is here for traffic because, without traffic, you can't do anything with your website, and this all comes when traffic alone is not responsible for SEO success strategy. Still, genuine traffic is the key to success. Not all users are on your website to read and know about you or your products and services, but most have come as an accidental search, referral, or backlink.

The traffic worthy of your attention is your genuine, unique recurrent user who intentionally came and stayed at your website. I have people land on my website, and they last for more than 10/15 minutes; this is genuine traffic I attracted to my content through different SEO strategies. So, make yourself an evaluation and monitor your recurring natural traffic and adjust your SEO strategy for people like them.

Suggestions to do better in your Traffic SEO Strategy:

Do It;

- Increase the quality and quantity of content you publish on your website
- Improve your local SEO to promote and share your content on multiple platforms, including social media
- Get the best backlinks for authority websites to have the juice to serve your users better through your content and SEO strategy

Don't Do It:

- Don't underestimate the power of on-page optimization
- Don't overestimate the ability of off-page optimization

- Don't forget to do your technical SEO
- Don't forget to have a perfect website structure to engage your users with better design and unique content

For User Satisfaction

User satisfaction is the only asset that will lead you to earn more links, content shares, and social media mentions. These are all practices that promote your content on different platforms to leverage the power of SEO to have greater user satisfaction through your content, design, and fast-loading website.

In the business world, the customer is everything; in the online website world, a satisfied user is everything; if you don't serve them well, they have countless opportunities to choose other sources for their information, education, and entertainment. Work on your user satisfaction by using SEO strategy and following suggestions to have positive results.

Suggestions to do better in your User Satisfaction SEO Strategy:

Do It;

- Invest time and resources in speed optimization of your blog and website
- Choose the title tags and meta description that sell your ideas to your users
- Optimization of your visual content like images and videos
- Make easy navigation for your user to go to their preferred sections on your website

Don't Do It:

- Don't get content from automated AI chatbots and assistants
- Don't use Flash or Java; if you do, it must be minimal
- Don't use pop-ups, under, and other intrusive ads; this lowers the users' satisfaction

- Don't get caught in redirects; this makes your website the hub of spammy content and comments

For Visibility

Visibility is your next opportunity to divert organic traffic into the recurring and repetitive genuine traffic you need for your growth and revenue. In Karachi, we have at least two advertising mantras on each billboard. The first one is "Fit hai tau Hit hai," meaning that if it is fit, it is hit. The second one is "Dekhegi tau Bikhegi"; if it is visible, it will sell.

These are both the perfect definitions of visibility. If your website fits and sounds in all the aspects of SEO and best content and delivery practices, then your website will be visible to your users. The second concept is that if it is visible, you can expect that your SEO is doing its best to get you the best results from search engines.

Suggestions to do better in your Visibility SEO Strategy:

Do It;

- Use psychological headlines
- Use awesome header tags and sub-tags to give your user a reason to explore further your website and its content
- Make sure your website is mobile-friendly because this is the dominant medium users use for their online searches
- Use the best optimizes images with alt tags for your websites; ensure it is yours and not a copyright free image
- Update your sitemap and submit it to search engines regularly
- Maintain your website daily for any code, theme, plugins, and integrations for upgradation

Don't Do It:

- Don't overdo psychological headlines if you are unfamiliar with the concept I coined in my book "The Psychological Headlines: **Creating compelling headlines**

for everything you want to write."
- Don't panic over creating fantastic headers and sub-tags
- Don't ignore mobile optimization of your website and mobile responsiveness
- Don't get others' images even if they have credited it copyright free
- Don't overdo your sitemap submission. I suggest submitting it after significant changes in your website structure, pages, and categories

CHAPTER 4: WHEN TO USE SEO

This question is one of the fundamental questions we are dealing with in this book about SEO basics. When must you do SEO? Well, there are many reasons to do it; however, what I consider the most important is when you are; claiming authority and expertise, doing the Best Research, Doing the Best to Serve Your User, Doing the Best Work, Doing The Right Thing Ethical, Engagement, Leadership, Leveraging Tech To Your Benefit, Market Share, Process Not The Destination, Thought Leadership.

In this chapter, you will find many essential insights and experience-based knowledge you can't find elsewhere. Here we go;

When Claiming Your Authority

Claiming authority is the number one aspect of SEO if you want to be an authority in your field. Authority has many metrics created by field experts, but the most critical element is publishing and putting it in front of the public and community-specific researchers and students. When you want to establish your authority in your field, you start posting your research and answering the students if they have questions about your topic of interest.

Your peers evaluate your research and give you solid suggestions about your research's weaknesses and strengths. Researchers in your field start replicating your methodology and recommend new aspects in your study; when you work on their recommendations, your research is more applicable and authentic, paving your path to authority in your field. The first reason you must use SEO is to claim your authority.

Suggestions to do better in your SEO Strategy when Claiming Your Authority:

Do It;

- Work on your website design and navigation
- Create content worth sharing
- Create original content you and your users need or prefer to read
- Update your information from authority sources
- Get the best tools and products supporting your authority
- Use your social media profiles to claim your authority

Don't Do It:

- Don't forget to work on your website's effectiveness and efficiency, especially on your visuals
- Don't expect instant results; Authority is a lonely way, and you have to pass silently, ensuring that you do not wake the giants along the way
- Don't ignore the quality: Focus on the quality of your content and improve the quality of backlinks
- Don't pass the copy-pasted content ever on your platforms, including your social media
- Don't take content and information from secondary sources if your aim is claiming and establishing your authority
- Don't share content you are not comfortable sharing on your website
- Don't stop updating your content on the regular basis
- Don't lose your originality in the rat race of SEO
- Don't use deceptive tools and products to rank higher; once discovered, you are gone forever
- Don't stay on Social media all the time; if you do, how can you establish your authority? My preferred use of Social media is 20 minutes in 24 hours. What is your use? It's up to you but doesn't overdo it. It will eat up all your free time that can be used on other essential tasks

When Claiming Your Expertise

Expertise is the technical aspect of authority; psychologically, authority is the perception, while expertise is the sensory part of the authority. You can see practically how one person is an expert in their field while observing their art and craft directly or indirectly.

You can see one's expertise while focusing on speed, accuracy, time spent on the task, research methods, use of tools, and asking for help when in need. Whenever you want to claim your authority, you must work on SEO to appear as an expert in your field and industry.

Suggestions to do better in your SEO Strategy When Claiming Your Expertise:

Do It;

- Work on your blog and pages, including your website's visual and logical navigational part
- Select quality authoritative websites and guest blogs on it
- Engage in online communities and share your expertise there
- Do it if you have time and energy to speak at local, national, and international conferences, seminars, workshops, and events. I have gone through all these, so I am sure of their effectiveness. Now I haven't time, so I have minimized my time on a handful of platforms and my entrepreneurial commitments to deliver to my students and clients worldwide through my courses and online academies
- Publish articles in local and international journals where your field experts find you and connect with you
- Webinars and podcasts, infographics, videos, and social media are your online mediums to connect with your users. Use them all wisely.
- Regularly keep an eye on your online reputation because expertise has another side to it, and it is creating enemies and rivalries online
- Make your content and website its design and navigation easy to use. You can refer to my website as a reference. I have given my users everything they want in one visit;
    1. Login: For my existing users, clients, and students; If they want to log in to resume their experience and search preferences, manage their memberships, continue their lessons, and read my latest blogs
    2. Subscription opportunity for new users; if they want to subscribe, they will not search for it; they can find it there. I also give them a subscription method to my blog by highlighting clearly; Subscribe to the blog via email.
    3. Search the topic of your choice: Allowing them to explore everything they wish to read on my website
    4. Google Translate: If they are not fully proficient in my written language: English, Pashto, and Urdu, respectively, they can translate my blogs and

website to their preferred language without searching for an online translator and going to and from my website to other websites. This is why my users stay on my website for longer than 15 to 20 minutes. Although translation is not 100% correct, they get the theme of my written work which is what I prefer over anything else
5. Most popular blogs: They can find my most popular blog posts that others are reading now. So, they can quickly scroll and choose what resonates with them and their hearts and minds
6. Need help? Let me know how I can help you in your business and life; this is my direct contact link; they can contact me whenever they need my help. I don't let my user search for my contact information, so they can contact me whenever they need my help.
7. Learn more by reading my blog; this is about all the blog categories I have published since 2003. Here my users choose their preferred category and start reading on.
8. Popular Courses: Here, I give my users a glimpse of the courses they can take to step into their future. I don't expect my users to search for my website navigation and find their way to my academy. Busy users don't have time to do it. My courses visibility tells them what I have in my academy
9. Search the Book of Your Choice: In the search bar, if they have read one of my Books' 2nd editions on Amazon, they are interested in reading the first publications, they either go to ANish Publications or get it on my website by simply searching the title here. Because I have dozens of books published on different topics over two decades in three languages, it won't be easy for them to search for their preferred book one by one.
10. Books Categories: If they are interested in a particular category and need that in my books, they can easily navigate through it.
11. Keywords: Here, I give my users all relevant keywords that they can find on my website
12. Stay Updated Via my social media platforms: Here, I give them more channels to be updated about my new blogs, books, courses, and other moments I share about my professional life
13. Follow Me On Twitter: Here, I give my users a way to get the free content I share on that platform

Don't Do It:

- Don't deceive others about your capabilities and potential
- Don't make false claims; be always honest personally and professionally
- Don't reinvent the wheel but stick to the basics of SEO
- Don't hate your critics and rivals; they can give you an idea that can create you a fortune. Sincerely listen to them and never say anything good or bad about them. I am practicing it to this day; that is why I am suggesting you too
- Don't comprise over the quality of your content, products, and services

- Please don't put your user experience on the bay; they can give you more insight than your critics, peers, and professional reviewers can ever give you
- Don't forget to analyze your content and website weekly and monthly
- Don't get discouraged when you see opposition
- Don't stop learning new things about your field from people of different backgrounds and expertise level

When Claiming Your Leadership

Leadership is an acquired skill; anyone with the ability to lead others can be a leader and authority in any field. Leadership is not management but leading others by your example; courageous individuals take this challenge and get their guts and grit to deliver excellent results to their respective users; the attitude, no matter what, plays a significant role in their leadership.

They take risks to impact the arena and accept responsibility for each action and decision. When you want to claim leadership in your field, you are ready to lose everything you have in pursuit of success. SEO is for you if you are prepared to invest your time, money, and resources to get the results. Get back and start working to deliver the best results you intend to provide to your users.

Suggestions to do better in your Leadership SEO Strategy:

Do It;

- Be aware of trends and developments in the field
- Take calculated risks to experiment with new techniques in SEO
- Have an open mind and a heart about the latest algorithmic changes in the search engines you use; I have installed five search engines on my mobile phone and more than 50 search engines on bookmarks. It's up to you to select and use and keep a constant check over their changes

Don't Do It:

- Don't risk your reputation
- Don't get bored with minimal procedures
- Don't overdo SEO so that you forget your most important task of creation and sharing

- Don't complicate things; keep your strategy simple and easy to replicate

When Leveraging Tech For Your Benefit

Do your best when you want to leverage tech for your benefit. Technology can help you in many things in your personal and professional lives. Still, one of your best benefits is using it for your branding, research, information, education, and entertainment. Here are some fantastic suggestions and recommendations for using SEO techniques.

Suggestions to do better in your SEO Strategy:

Do It;

- Use natural language to have genuine traffic to your website
- Use powerful words to attract users to your content
- Use grammar-checking software and services online to better your content and make it grammatically sound and well researched
- Use plagiarism checks for possible plagiarism issues

Don't Do It:

- Do not use synonyms if you don't need them in your content; although grammatical software is not fond of the exact words, there are essential concepts that synonyms can miss, and the user will lose interest in your content
- Don't misspell; use plurals, numbers, and symbols in your keywords; they can end up in penalization by search engines, and you will lose ranking as well as users

When Claiming Your Market Share

Start doing SEO instantly when you want to claim a Market share. This goal has a lot to pay attention to; once you claim it, you can't back down. Market share is for industry leaders; if you claim it, you have to prove it.

First, to yourself, then others; it is better to use SEO to help you get results worth achieving. Here are some suggestions and recommendations that helped me claim my market share in a local and international market, and I am sure it will help you claim yours.

Suggestions to do better in your SEO Strategy:

Do It;

- Improve your website content, design, visuals, and aesthetics
- Attract your genuine traffic through your authentic content and sincere help
- Optimize your website for screens adjustments and mobile friendliness
- Enhance your website speed and make easier your navigation

Don't Do It:

- Be patient enough to claim and expand your market share; it needs time, resources, education, and a proper mindset
- Focus on one industry or market; either work on digital services and products or physical doesn't work in both markets
- Don't be the one-stop place for everything for everyone
- Improve your customers' service
- Word of mouth rules the world; use it in your favor
- Allocate proper budget for SEO strategy and marketing processes
- Constantly testing and permanently be closing

When Claiming Your Thought Leadership

Get the best results from your SEO strategy by claiming our thought leadership. In ancient times when you wanted to become a leader, you would gather an army and claim your leadership. Time went by, and now with the advanced technology, you need the right tools to earn your position by researching, creating content, and delivering it to the right people at the right time. You get your unclaimed territory of thought leadership. Here are some suggestions and recommendations for your way toward the top.

Suggestions to do better in your SEO Strategy:

Do It;

- Creating and maintaining a blog is your valuable asset in the long run. I have been managing my blog for more than two decades, and I can't imagine whatever I have received in my life and profession would ever be possible without the help of my blog. Even this book and all my books on ANish publications and now on Amazon publishing are the results of my blog. My blog has a trace of everything I have ever created.
- Speak at seminars, workshops, and conferences
- Maintain your social media profiles and engage with your like-minded friends, colleagues, and dedicated users
- Write in industry publications articles, thought pieces, and on trendy topics; you might like to be considered a leader in
- Conduct and publish interviews
- Be on industry boards or committees; I started as president of the students' affairs committee in the department of Psychology, then Martial in Scouts Group, senior writer, researcher, and psychologist. A serial entrepreneur and cofounder… my journey continue. Be in leadership roles to be a thought leader in your field
- Write a book on your industry pain points and deliver solutions to the burning issues of your industry
- Create a YouTube channel or podcast to host a program so your users can get to know you and your valuable thoughts as soon as possible.

Don't Do It:

- Please don't ignore your audience and their genuine suggestions and recommendations
- Don't give your website outdated; update your audience with your thoughts regularly
- Don't underestimate the power of your social media game plan
- Don't get stuck in poor-quality content and SEO strategy
- Never lose your originality and individuality
- Don't get discouraged by the naysayers, and encourage others
- Don't lose hope if you encounter opposition from small minds; it's a rule of this game

CHAPTER 5: SEO BASICS: WHERE TO USE SEO

Where to use SEO? This question is one of the basics that beginners, intermediate, and advanced-level SEOs ask me whenever I come in contact with them. And my answer always includes one of the following aspects of SEO strategy:

For Awareness

Awareness is the first step of SEO, which starts your game plan. Your SEO is your refuge for awareness because no one knows precisely online who you are, what you do, and how you do it. To introduce your brand and website, you need the following suggestion to use SEO strategy to impact the online world.

Suggestions to do better in your Awareness SEO Strategy:

Do It;

- Ensure the quality of your content
- Ensure the quality of your links internally and externally
- Improve website security
- Enhance its speed and accuracy
- Be consistent in your content creation and publications
- Get the best themes, plugins, and tools to monitor your progress and users engagement

Don't Do It:

- Don't mislead your users with inaccurate titles and tags
- Don't create and publish thin content full of irrelevant keywords
- Don't believe in conspiracy theories that will get you penalized for disinformation and misleading behaviors

For Education

The second aspect of where to use SEO is education. Education is the core factor of SEO, whether it is educating users about your products and services or machine learning models of AI. SEO is your first help to rescue you and your website from the manipulation of disinformation. Here are some suggestions and recommendations for the betterment of educational aspects of SEO.

Suggestions to do better in your SEO Strategy:

Do It;

- Create content about your products and services to educate your users
- Infographic is your friend for showing your users what the main point of your products and service is
- Create visuals like videos and graphic representations on your website
- Create and update your FAQs page and answer all possible questions your target audience may have about our products and services
- Use the power of case studies and success stories about people who have used your products and services
- Offer introductory lower fees of membership on your website
- Give discounts to your users on special occasions
- Create online courses to educate your users about your field and their interest-based industry-specific domain

Don't Do It:

- Don't overdo excessive links in your content
- Don't lie to your users via your content

For Social Media

Connection is the currency of social media; you connect with your users and followers. SEO is fundamental to your success on social media platforms and your website. Your user goes to social media from your website, and your target users come to your website. Here are some suggestions and recommendations for your success on social media via SEO.

Suggestions to do better in your Social media SEO Strategy:

Do It;

- Work on creating a connection with your users and customers
- Work on sharing relevant and attractive content to increase engagement
- Network with industry experts
- Be updated about your industry news and trends
- Share your audiovisuals on social media
- Drive traffic to your website via social media
- Generate leads from social media
- Build online reputation and brand awareness on social media

Don't Do It:

- Don't do duplication of content, products, and services
- Don't promote irrelevant content
- Don't post poorly written content that is not engaging, visually attractive, and shareable
- Don't post if it hasn't, and Call to Action in it

CHAPTER 6: SEO BASICS: WHICH TYPE OF SEO

SEO is of different types depending on its content and context, including but not limited to on-page SEO, off-page SEO, National SEO, International SEO, and Technical SEO, to name a few.

Each type of SEO is made for its special delivery and feature that can help you boost your search ranking and increase traffic. Below are given types of SEO along with suggestions and recommendations to give you a fantastic experience through your SEO journey.

On-Page Seo

On-page SEO is related to everything you have to offer on webpages, including but not limited to titles, meta tags, and descriptions for your pages, alt tags for your images, anchor text for your links, headings, and subheadings, content throughout your pages, mobile-first indexing, structured data, fast and responsive design. Here are some recommendations and suggestions to get the most out of your on-page SEO.

Suggestions to do better in your On-Page SEO Strategy:

Do It;

- Work on keyword-specific titles that can attract your target audience to your website
- Invest your time and efforts in writing your keywords-based meta tags for your content, blogs, and website pages
- Your description must include your keywords
- Never forget to use alt tags for images
- Enhance your anchor text for all your links
- Write your headings and subheadings around your keywords
- Create quality, keyword-dense content
- Make your website mobile friendly
- Build your website on structured data to improve your chances of ranking
- Work on your speed and responsiveness to give an excellent experience to your users

Don't Do It:

- Don't stuff, repeat, or overdo your keywords in your titles, descriptions, tags, anchor texts, alt texts, and content

Off-Page Seo

Off-page means everything that has nothing to do with your on-page SEO strategy. This type of SEO is mainly used in earning and building backlinks. A few suggestions about it include;

Suggestions to do better in your SEO Strategy:

Do It;

- Earn links from authoritative websites
- Devise a link-building strategy and don't violate the best practices of link building
- Make good relationships with your other websites' admins; they can help you in earning more quality links for them and their other friends

Don't Do It:

- Don't buy or sell links
- Don't engage in link farms

- Never involved in link-back schemes
- Don't get automated links

Technical Seo

Technical SEO is another essential type of SEO that focuses on your website's design, code, speed, quality, and quantity of backlinks, ranking, XML sitemaps, and redirects. Although none of these factors directly impact SEO but indirectly make it impossible to run for a long time. Some of the suggestions and recommendations include the following;

Suggestions to do better in your SEO Strategy:

Do It;

- Analyze your website's overall design, code, and loading speed
- Research and select high-quality keywords for your content
- Enhance your title tags, meta descriptions, and other aspects of your content
- Improve the quality and quantity of links to your website
- Remove or replace broken links
- Create XML sitemaps and submit them to search engines

Don't Do It:

- Technical SEO is as crucial as On-page and off-page, so you can't ignore it
- Don't ever let your website design, code, or loading speed scare away your users
- Don't use keyword stuffing, hidden texts or links, cloaking, doorway pages, link farms, and black SEO tactics

CHAPTER 7: SEO BASICS: HOW TO DO SEO

This question is equally important while working on your SEO strategy especially starting with your keywords, Titles, URLs, Meta Descriptions, H1 Texts, Page Contents, Link Building, Social Media, Monitoring for good and bad practices, Trends, and Their Lives, Images, and Site Design Structures.

In this chapter, I will suggest and recommend many things to answer the question of How-to SEO.

Start with Keywords and Suggestions to do better in your Keywords SEO Strategy:

Do It;

- Research and choose your keywords wisely
- Optimize and promote your keywords
- Utilize social media keywords and tags

Don't Do It:

- Avoid stuffing your keywords
- Avoid irrelevant keywords

Then Do your Titles SEO and Suggestions to do better in your Titles SEO Strategy:

Do It;

- Write concise and clear titles for your blogs and pages
- Utilize your keywords wisely on your website
- Write psychological titles
- Get unique titles every time you write your content

Don't Do It:

- Don't start your titles with stop words
- Don't stuff your title with your keywords
- Don't write very short or long titles
- Don't create duplicate titles with spinning keywords and synonyms

Then Do your URL SEO; here are a few suggestions to do better in your URL Strategy:

Do It;

- Make your URL concise and straightforward so your users can easily remember it
- Make your URL relevant to your keywords
- For separating words, use hyphens
- Always write in lowercase
- Never use special characters

Don't Do It:

- Don't write long, complicated, too general, or specific
- Avoid writing special characters in URLs
- Don't use one keyword twice in the URLs

Suggestions to do better in your Meta Descriptions SEO Strategy:

Do It;

- Your Meta description should be between 80-120 characters

- Use relevant keywords in your Meta descriptions
- Write in Active voice
- Write in sentence cases, avoid duplications in the meta descriptions

Don't Do It:

- Avoid creating generic meta descriptions
- Avoid misleading, irrelevant, and poorly written meta descriptions

CHAPTER 8: SEO BASICS: WHO SHOULD DO SEO?

Everyone interested in having an impact on internet at local and international level. Still following people qualify for having the best SEO strategy to survive the internet strom not having mercy for anyone at any level.

1. **Creative** individuals /teams/ startups/ companies/ corporations
2. **Genuine** individuals /teams/ startups/ companies/ corporations
3. **Honest** individuals /teams/ startups/ companies/ corporations

SEO BASICS GUIDELINES

- Research and select keyword research tools
- Utilize Analytics tools to gauge your progress and performance
- Read and join industry-standard blogs, forums, groups, and comminutes
- Never hesitate to research and experiment with your SEO techniques and strategies
- Join all significant social media platforms and connect with your target audience
- Set higher standards of quality and quantity for your blog and website content
- Monitor your performance regularly
- Create better internal and external links

SEO BASICS CHECKLIST

- Ensure your website is optimized and accessible to both users and search engines
- Enhance your website visibility
- Create the best content that you like to share with the world
- Utilize robots.txt to manage which areas should be accessible to search engines

CHAPTER 9: SUGGESTIONS AND RECOMMENDATIONS

For Beginners

- Work on your research skills and start playing with your keywords and content but wisely
- Increase your website's visibility
- Optimize your content for better ranking
- Promote your content on social media
- Improve your back-linking strategies
- Familiarize yourself with analytics and marketing tools
- Keep your website fresh by supplying the best content you can create
- Ask for help when you need it from your seniors and pros in SEOs

For Intermediate Level Seos

- Improve your content with better keywords
- Write better-quality blog posts that your users want to read
- Improve your social media engagement
- Work to make your website mobile responsive
- Enhance your website speed and minimize your website's loading time
- Utilize schema markup to improve your website structure
- Check your progress regularly

For Advanced Level Seos

- Enhance your website content by focusing on topics and keywords that have the potential for better ranking in the long run
- Deep research your keywords and your target audience; what are their pinpoints
- Look for the existing content for repurposing and opportunities to improve its ranking

- Optimize your title tags, meta descriptions, on-page, off-page, and technical SEO to increase your chances of visibility
- Link building is a strategy that needs time and effort, and better content to earn links worthy of keeping
- Monitor your progress by setting clear-cut KPIs for better evaluations
- Utilize free and paid tools to check your analytics, new trends, and behavioral change in your user engagement with your website content

UP TO YOU, DEAR READER!

Upto You And Suggestions For Your Success In Seo

- Ensure your website's design and easy navigation
- Utilize the power of psychological headlines for better ranking and visibility
- Use analytics to monitor your progress
- Make your website mobile friendly
- Leverage Social media to your benefit
- Earn links from higher authority websites
- Work on your content marketing to improve your branding and search engines visibility
- Not doing keyword research
- Not getting help from tools for analytics and monitoring
- Not implementing popular search engines' best guidelines for better ranking opportunities
- Not working for improvements in knowledge and experience
- Create the mindset of a warrior and experiment with the SEO techniques you learned from this book
- Make sure you make it a habit to take the next step after the first one
- Invest time and effort in researching and creating better-quality content
- You can make it; the future is yours to achieve success

ACKNOWLEDGEMENT

I acknowledge all those who were there for me, either online or offline, who gave me hope and strength to complete my book with everything I have in mind. I wish them all the best and hope they will forgive any errors I have made in the book and let me know what they think about my book immediately without hesitation. I love you all, and I hope for your success too.

ABOUT THE AUTHOR

Ali Muattar

Ali Muattar is one of the most valued authors on our platform, making everything to leverage us the best results from search engines worldwide and working on our IT projects since the beginning of the IT department to complete our indigenous search engine driven by our database having everything we have at our online and offline data files.

This book is by a seasoned marketer and cyber security expert, unveiling the SEO community's secrets and sharing his insights with beginners on leveraging it for your benefit. We wish you good luck. We hope for the best for you guys to take something from this book and use it for you and your online presence.

This book is the first in the ANish Publications SEO series, following the SEO Best Practices: For Experts and Advanced Level Professionals, SEO Best Practices for Beginners, and Search Engine Optimization: Writing Techniques for New Writers. We suggest you read it too.

Enjoy your reading journey ahead.

ANISH PUBLICATIONS' SEO SERIES

This book is the first in the ANish Publications' SEO series, following the SEO Best Practices: For Experts and Advanced Level Professionals, SEO Best Practices for Beginners, and Search Engine Optimization: Writing Techniques for New Writers. We suggest you read it too. Enjoy your reading journey ahead.

Seo Best Practices: For Experts And Advanced Level Professionals

SEO Best Practices For Experts And Advanced Level Professionals, Every field has the best practices to operate. The scientific community calls for ethics in the area, and in the field of SEO, there is also a need for better ways to increase traffic to your company website. The author has served many clients for years in diverse industries worldwide. He has also written SEO Basics, SEO Writing Techniques, and SEO best practices for content. He has SEO best practices for Copywriting to generate traffic to your business website and convert visitors into customers. If you are interested in self and career improvements, this book will help you see the results yourself.

Seo Best Practices For Beginners

SEO Best Practices For Beginners Every field has the best practices to operate. The scientific community calls it ethics of the area, and for the field of SEO, there is also a need for the best ways to increase traffic to your company website. The author has been serving many clients for years in diverse industries worldwide. He has also written SEO Basics, SEO Writing Techniques, and SEO best practices for content. He has SEO best practices for Copywriting to generate traffic to your business website and convert visitors into customers. If you are interested in self and career improvements, this book will help you see the results yourself.

Search Engine Optimization: Writing Techniques For New Writers

Search Engine Optimization Writing Techniques For New Writers SEO is a fact and reality because, apart from advertisement and marketing, you have little to no advantage over billions of websites searching for audience attention and focus like you. What can you do? Cry and whine, or try and shine? The choice is yours. The hard workers stand last and win, but the intelligent workers earn fast; this is the brutal reality of today's online and digital world. As a chief SEO manager at some well-known brands and businesses having successful e-commerce websites, the author of this book learned many ways to optimize your content and copy for search engines. The constant change in search engines' algorithms pushes managers to act quickly and efficiently. If you want to use current, necessary, and essential SEO techniques, this book will grasp the crucial aspects of writing content and copy for your website and your client's websites and stores.

THE END

www.ingramcontent.com/pod-product-compliance
Lightning Source LLC
Chambersburg PA
CBHW051201220526
45473CB00003B/858